THE BULLY-FREE ZONE

WHEN PEOPLE BULLY IN GROUPS

THERESE HARASYMIW

PowerKiDS
press™
New York

Published in 2021 by The Rosen Publishing Group, Inc.
29 East 21st Street, New York, NY 10010

First Edition

Portions of this work were originally authored by Addy Ferguson and published as *Group Bullying: Exclusion and Ganging Up*. All new material in this edition was authored by Therese Harasymiw.

Editor: Therese Shea
Book Design: Reann Nye

Photo Credits: Cover SpeedKingz/Shutterstock.com; series art Here/Shutterstock.com; p. 4 Syda Productions /Shutterstock.com; pp. 5, 11 Monkey Business Images/Shutterstock.com; p. 7 Tom Wang/ Shutterstock.com; p. 9 Pixel-Shot/Shutterstock.com; p. 10 Brocreative/Shutterstock.com; p. 13 Kevin Dodge/Getty Images; p. 14 Rawpixel.com/Shutterstock.com; p. 15 fstop123/E+/Getty Images; p. 17 © iStockphoto.com/kali9; p. 19 Cavan Images/Cavan/Getty Images; p. 20 SDI Productions/E+/Getty Images; p. 21 ONOKY - Brooke Auchincloss/Brand X Pictures/Getty Images; p. 22 FatCamera/E+/Getty Images.

Library of Congress Cataloging-in-Publication Data

Names: Harasymiw, Therese, author.
Title: When people bully in groups / Therese Harasymiw.
Description: New York : PowerKids Press, [2021] | Series: The bully-free zone | Includes index.
Identifiers: LCCN 2019059518 | ISBN 9781725319486 (paperback) | ISBN 9781725319509 (library binding) | ISBN 9781725319493 (6 pack)
Subjects: LCSH: Bullying–Juvenile literature.
Classification: LCC BF637.B85 H355 2021 | DDC 302.34/3–dc23
LC record available at https://lccn.loc.gov/2019059518

Manufactured in the United States of America

Some of the images in this book illustrate individuals who are models. The depictions do not imply actual situations or events.

CPSIA Compliance Information: Batch #CSPK20. For Further Information contact Rosen Publishing, New York, New York at 1-800-237-9932.

Find us on

CONTENTS

THE DEFINITION OF BULLYING

Have you ever been bullied? Have you known someone who has been bullied? If you have, you have an idea of what it is. U.S. government groups came together to write an exact **definition**. They stated that bullying is an **aggressive** and harmful way of acting among school-aged children. Bullying is hurting someone's body, using harmful words against them, or leaving them out on purpose. Bullying happens more than once or is expected to continue.

IN THE ZONE

The U.S. government doesn't have any national laws against bullying itself. However, there are laws against bothering or attacking people because of their color, **disability,** and certain other features.

Bullying is often talked about as a problem among kids. However, kids who bully sometimes learn from adult bullies!

Bullying isn't always one person against another. Sometimes people bully together as a group. This book takes a look at what's behind group bullying and how to fight it.

DIFFERENT BULLYING, DIFFERENT BULLIES

People bully in different ways. Physical bullies use their bodies to hurt others, such as pushing, tripping, and hitting them. Using words to hurt others is called verbal bullying. Those who bully in this way might say things that hurt others' feelings or scare them.

Cyberbullies use words too. However, they use the internet and smartphones to spread their harmful messages. Some bullies leave people out of activities or out of their group on purpose. This is called social bullying. Social bullies may also do things such as tell unkind or **embarrassing** stories about their victim.

IN THE ZONE

The different kinds of bullying may mix. Verbal and social bullying also can be cyberbullying, for example.

All bullying is unkind,
wrong, and harmful.

HARMFUL BEHAVIORS, HARMFUL EFFECTS

Every kind of bullying does damage, or harm. The effects can last long after the bullying stops. Think about how you would feel if a group of girls and boys laughed every time you walked by, made fun of your clothes, or wouldn't let you hang out with them.

You might start worrying about what you look like or what people think of you. You might feel **depressed** or angry. You may try to skip school to avoid the bullies. Bullying can go beyond bad feelings as well. People who are bullied may have health problems such as headaches.

IN THE ZONE

Some kids who are bullied become bullies to others. A small number become **violent.**

Kids who are bullied may want to spend more time alone. They may miss school on purpose, which can affect their grades.

INSIDE A CLIQUE

In most schools, there are groups of students who spend a lot of their free time together. Sometimes these groups are open to new people joining them. Other times they aren't. A group that leaves out other people on purpose is called a clique (KLIHK).

IN THE ZONE

People in a clique may act how the others are acting because they don't want to be kicked out. That may mean bullying even if they really don't want to.

Kids enjoy hanging out in groups. However, a healthy group of friends allows those in it to be themselves and have other friends.

Cliques often have leaders. The others in the group want to please the leaders and fit in. To belong to the clique, they may not be allowed to have outside friends. They may have to dress or act in a certain way too. That may include bullying certain kids who are outside the group.

HOW CLIQUES BULLY

One way cliques bully is by excluding, or leaving out, others. They make it seem like someone isn't good enough to join the group. They may share embarrassing facts that make them think that or say untrue things about the person. The bullies also may just **ignore** the victim, which is hurtful too.

Cliques sometimes gang up on someone. They may tease or even physically hurt the person in some way. It's hard enough facing one bully. A whole group of bullies is even worse. Even if the entire group isn't bullying at the same time, it can feel like that to the victim.

IN THE ZONE

Bullies often like an **audience.** These people seem to be supporting the bully's actions.

WHY KIDS IN CLIQUES BULLY:

- To get attention
- To feel popular
- To feel powerful

- **Jealousy**
- To follow others
- Out of fear

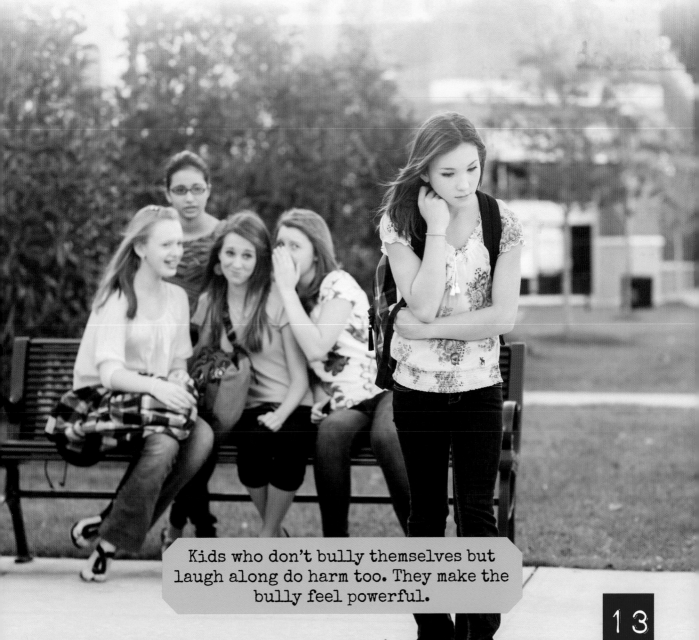

Kids who don't bully themselves but laugh along do harm too. They make the bully feel powerful.

13

COMBATTING A CLIQUE

When a group is ganging up on you, the best thing to do is walk away. If you can firmly tell them to leave you alone, do it. However, you don't want to sound like you're scared or upset. Bullies want a **reaction**, so it's best not to give one. Ignoring may end the bullying too.

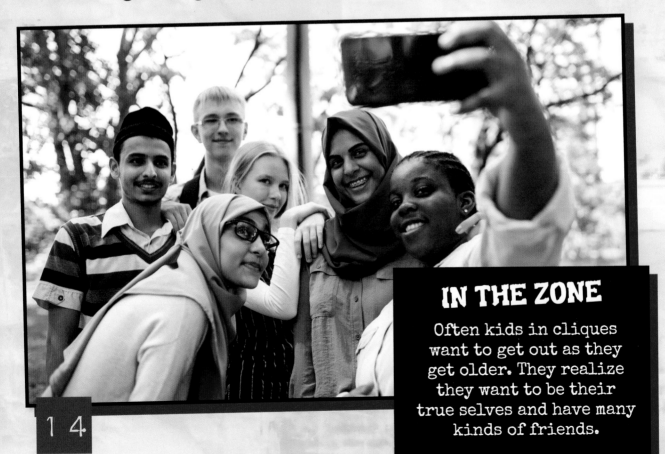

IN THE ZONE

Often kids in cliques want to get out as they get older. They realize they want to be their true selves and have many kinds of friends.

You may think you want to be in a clique. However, many kids in a clique are scared to act like themselves. You don't want friends who won't let you be yourself.

If people in a clique are pushing or hitting you, don't get into a fight. This can make the bullying worse. Fighting can also get you hurt or in trouble. You can help yourself or other victims of a bullying clique by seeking help.

GETTING HELP

One of the reasons bullying is so common is that victims don't tell anyone. They might think no one can or will help them. They might be afraid the bullying will get worse. They might be embarrassed or not want to talk about their bad feelings.

However, this is a mistake. Don't keep bullying to yourself, whether it's happening to you or someone else. Tell a trusted adult, such as a parent or teacher. They can help put a stop to the bullying. They can help you deal with your feelings of anger, sadness, fear, or shame. That's just as important.

If you think a clique is bullying someone, tell an adult. Whether you're inside or outside the group, you'll be helping someone.

KNOW YOURSELF, BE YOURSELF

Being bullied by a group of people feels terrible. It's hard to ignore. Sometimes, people who are bullied think it's their own fault. They think they should fit in so bullies don't pick on them. It's never their fault though.

The way we feel about ourselves is called self-esteem. Don't allow bullies to hurt your self-esteem. Make new friendships with people who like you for your true self. One way to do this is to find groups of people who have the same interests as you. These groups might have to do with sports, hobbies, or **volunteering**.

IN THE ZONE

Some kids who are bullied will need to talk to a counselor. A counselor's job is to listen and give advice. Bullies need counselors to learn how to stop too.

Turn an interest in helping others into a way of making new friends. That's a great way to feel better about yourself.

BATTLING BULLIES IN SCHOOL

Most bullying takes place in school. Many schools have decided to take action against bullying. The students agree to make their school a bully-free zone, where all kids can feel safe. Every student needs to speak out when they see bullying happening. Kids who have been bullied report that having other kids stand up for them was the most helpful way to stop the bullying.

IN THE ZONE

Even kids who just witness bullying can suffer harmful effects. It helps everyone when schools put a stop to bullying.

Successful anti-bullying programs teach kids to have **empathy** for each other. We treat each other better when we try to understand how others feel.

If your school doesn't have an anti-bullying program, you and your friends could start one. Talk to a teacher or your principal about your idea. Putting an end to bullying could start with you!

IT'S ABOUT RESPECT

If you or someone you know is being bullied, there are lots of places to turn to for help. Websites such as the U.S. government's Stopbullying.gov can give you more facts. The National Bullying Prevention Center's site www.pacer.org/bullying offers tips for stopping bullying. Teachers and counselors at your school may have had training about how to stop it too.

Whether the bullying comes from a single person or a group, it's wrong. Everyone deserves to be treated with respect. That's how bullying stops. You and your classmates can encourage others to stop standing by and start standing up against bullying!

GLOSSARY

aggressive: Showing a readiness to attack or do harm.

audience: A group of people who gather together to watch something.

definition: An explanation of the meaning of a word.

depressed: Feeling sad, hopeless, or unimportant.

disability: A problem that makes it difficult for a person to do certain things.

embarrassing: Causing somebody to be ashamed or ill at ease.

empathy: A feeling of understanding and sharing in another person's experiences and emotions.

ignore: To do nothing about or in response to something. Also, to pretend not to notice.

jealousy: An unhappy feeling of wanting what someone else has.

reaction: The way someone acts or feels in response to something that happens.

violent: Using physical force to cause harm or damage to someone or something.

volunteering: Doing work without getting paid or being asked to do it.

INDEX

WEBSITES

Due to the changing nature of Internet links, PowerKids Press has developed an online list of websites related to the subject of this book. This site is updated regularly. Please use this link to access the list: www.powerkidslinks.com/bullyfree/groups